SUPERSTARS OF FILM

robert de niro

Elfreda Powell

CHELSEA HOUSE PUBLISHERS
Philadelphia

First published in traditional hardback edition
© 1998 by Chelsea House Publishers.
Printed in Hong Kong
Copyright © Parragon Book Service Ltd 1995
Unit 13–17, Avonbridge Trading Estate, Atlantic Road
Avonmouth, Bristol, England BS11 9QD

Library of Congress Cataloging-in-Publication Data
Powell, Elfreda.
    Robert De Niro / by Elfreda Powell.
        p.   cm. — (Superstars of film)
    Originally published : London : Parragon Books, 1996.
    Includes index.
    Filmography: p.
    Summary: A biography of the Hollywood legend known for
his ability to change totally with every role, donning that
persona and becoming the one he portrays.
    ISBN 0-7910-4645-1 (hardcover)
    1, De Niro, Robert—Juvenile literature.   2. Motion picture
actors and actresses—United States—Biography—Juvenile
literature.
    [1. De Niro, Robert.   2. Actors and actresses.]   I.Title.
    II.Series.
    PN2287.D37P68   1997
    791.43'028'092—dc21
    [B]   97-22648
                                                           CIP
                                                           AC

ACKNOWLEDGMENTS
AIP (courtesy Kobal)
Aquarius
Columbia (courtesy Kobal)
EMI/Columbia/Warners (courtesy Kobal)
Paramount (courtesy Kobal)
Taplin-Perry-Scorsese (courtesy Kobal)
TriBeCa/Cecchi Gori/Berlusconi (courtesy Kobal)
United Artists (courtesy Kobal)
Universal (courtesy Kobal)
Warner Bros. (courtesy Kobal)

CONTENTS

As the police photographer in Mad Dog and Glory

"The fathomless deep. Huge emotions right under the sur-face," is how Meryl Streep describes his eyes. Dark, enig-matic, and brooding, Robert is one of America's finest con-temporary actors and has been compared to both Marlon Brando and Alec Guinness. He chooses his roles with care: his characters come from the flip side of the American Dream, from the urban underworld, the garishly lit streets, the boxing ring, the casino, the heist. They are people who live on the edge, in a world of violence.

De Niro is a perfectionist. He becomes his role with total commitment, then stands back slightly and relaxes so that after his performance we emerge from the movie thinking and seeing the way *his* characters think and see.

On the subject of his private life, he is reserved. *Newsweek* magazine called him a "black hole." His evasive interviews give almost nothing away. His family life is kept secret; his circle of friends is small. He does not want to be recognized on the street.

Director Brian De Palma calls him "a chameleon," for his ability to change totally with every role, donning the persona, *becoming* the person, so much so that we might be forgiven for asking: Who is the real De Niro?

DeNiro (far right) played one of Shelley Winters's sons in Bloody Mama

A LONELY CHILDHOOD

Robert De Niro grew up in New York's Greenwich Village. His father, who had the same name, was born in Syracuse, New York, of an Italian father and Irish mother. Robert De Niro, Sr., was an idealist, a painter of such high standards that before he would sell a painting, he had to think that the buyer was worthy of buying it. Consequently much of his life was spent in poverty. He had studied painting with noted Abstract Expressionist painter Hans Hofmann, who had fled to the United States from Nazi Germany and become the central figure in the contemporary art movement on the East Coast. In these painting classes De Niro Sr. met his future wife, Virginia Admiral, an equally talented painter from Oregon. They fell in love, married, and went to live in Greenwich Village, at that time a lively center of bohemian life.

Their only child, Robert (or Bobby, as he is generally known), was born on August 17, 1943. By all accounts they were a happy but rather intense couple who participated in the life around them. Greenwich Village was full of struggling artists like themselves, would-be writers and musicians, actors and intellectuals, as well as the usual number of fakes. They were to meet their nemesis in one of the latter— a quack psychoanalyst who persuaded them, as he had persuaded a number of other couples, that they were not really happy together and should split up. So when De Niro was only two years old, his parents went their separate ways.

His father continued to live from hand to mouth, struggling to make his way as an artist, moving from one dank loft to another; his mother, however, could no longer afford such an idealized way of life—she had to earn some money. She started her own small business, doing secretarial work and proofreading. Robert's parents' separation was not rancorous, and they continued to be on reasonable terms, although they officially divorced when Robert was only four, in 1948.

With his mother preoccupied with her work and with no siblings for company, Robert was a solitary child, very reliant on his own resources. He enjoyed reading, and also looked forward to the time he spent with his father, which, by all accounts, included visits to movies. His father had a volatile personality, and the high standards he demanded of himself were also extended to those around him. De Niro's own perfectionism as an actor undoubtedly had its roots in his relationship with his father. When Bobby was eight, his father disappeared completely from his life for four years. (He had decided to try to make his living as an artist in postwar France, but had no more success there than he had in New York.)

Bobby attended the local school in Greenwich Village. He was reputedly very shy and introverted, and fared only moderately well in class. He often skipped school but he didn't join any street gangs and certainly wasn't tough—he preferred reading a book. He was persuaded to take part in the school play, leading to his first public appearance as an actor—as the Cowardly Lion in *The Wizard of Oz*. Putting on a disguise can be a way for a shy child to gain courage, and this was obviously something he enjoyed.

One of Virginia De Niro's clients ran a famous drama school, the Dramatic Workshop. Directed by Erwin and Marie Ley Piscator, the school had seen many celebrated actors pass through its doors, including Marlon Brando in the early 1940s; by the 1950s Brando was mesmerizing audiences with his performances. At the age of ten, Bobby enrolled in the school's speech and drama classes.

By the time he was thirteen, his mother could afford to send him to a private school, but he still didn't shine academically and left at sixteen. He seemed to know exactly what he wanted to do—to act in films. He had apparently been inspired not so much by actors of the moment such as Brando, Montgomery Clift, and James Dean, but by the films *Can-Can, The Thing,* and *Invasion of the Body Snatchers*. He joined the Stella Adler Conservatory of Acting to further his dream and studied there for three years.

Stella Adler had worked at the Piscators' school and was a wonderful teacher. Brando acknowledges her as the most formative influence in his life. She had studied under Stanislavsky at the Moscow Arts Theatre and brought his technique of method acting back to the States. Brando was the first to bring method acting successfully to the screen in *The Men* and *A Streetcar Named Desire,* and all aspiring actors were now copying his technique. Adler taught actors to study outward clues to the character they were playing, and to replicate the character's emotions by looking inward to find parallel emotions or situations in their past to provoke similar reactions. She taught restrained vocal expression and advocated understatement—a subtlety in technique much suited to the screen and one that would revolutionize filmmaking.

Adler's rival in the teaching of method acting, Lee Strasberg, had established himself at the Actors Studio, where De Niro next attended workshop sessions but never enrolled as a student. Strasberg laid even more emphasis on using past feelings and past experiences to conjure up the emotions of a character, and De Niro was able to plunder his painful past to good effect. Strasberg immediately recognized his talent and encouraged it, although it would be many years before De Niro achieved public recognition.

De Niro with Jeanne Moreau in The Last Tycoon

WAITING IN THE WINGS

De Niro continued living in the Greenwich Village area, although it had lost its former bohemian glamour. His father had returned to France but was found to be living at starvation level, so Bobby set off for Paris to bring him home. He says little about this episode except that it was "a nightmare." His mother, on the other hand, had taken up painting again and was now having some success. The Museum of Modern Art in New York would eventually buy one of her paintings—no small achievement.

In the early 1960s Bobby managed to get his first film audition, with Brian De Palma, for *The Wedding Party*, although it would not be the break he was hoping for. Though De Palma found him intensely shy he did offer him a small part. De Niro gladly accepted it, thinking that the salary was $50 a week, and not, as it turned out, a flat fee of $50 for several weeks' filming. Worse still, the film would not be released for another six years, when it promptly sank without trace.

De Niro didn't make another film for some years, and in the meantime he worked hard at perfecting his craft. A girlfriend, Sally Kirkland, said that he had created a portfolio of twenty-five very different characters whose inspiration had come from novels he'd read. And he took part in any small theater production that he could find: from Chekhov and

Eugene O'Neill to a German Expressionist play. One of his more fascinating theater appearances was in *Glory, Glamour and Gold*, a production well Off-Broadway featuring Candy Darling, a transvestite friend of the Pop artist Andy Warhol. While Candy did Marilyn Monroe impersonations, De Niro partnered him/her in no less than five different roles.

After this De Niro took another trip to Europe—this time hitchhiking in search of his Irish and Italian roots. He managed to track down the Italian side of his family in the hill town of Campobasso, some fifty miles from Naples. When he returned to New York he made his second appearance on film—in a walk-on part in Marcel Carné's *Trois Chambres à Manhattan*, and not long after that was invited by Brian De Palma to take part in two further unmemorable counterculture films: *Greetings* and its sequel, *Hi, Mom!* In the first he played someone pretending to be a right-wing militant to avoid being called up for service in Vietnam (the war was by then in its third year). He changed his physical appearance so successfully that De Palma failed to recognize him. In *Hi, Mom!* he became a voyeur.

Although De Niro was still reserved and self-effacing, once he had immersed himself in his role, he was transformed. He saw life entirely through the eyes of his character. It was as though acting gave him permission to do things he would never dare to do himself. And De Palma encouraged him to improvise.

Sally Kirkland introduced him to Shelley Winters, by then a well-established star who had made some films. She took him under her wing, becoming a true, lifelong friend. She obtained a part for him in a satirical play, as a bisexual method actor who is also a karate expert. De Niro took karate training for three weeks, and by the time the play was staged he could chop a piece of wood in half with his bare hand. Although the play was a flop, De Niro was noticed.

Several more "dogs" followed—*Sam's Song, Jennifer on My Mind, Born to Win,* and *The Gang That Couldn't Shoot*

Straight. In the last of these he played what was for him a seminal role—an Italian gangster. Scrupulous in his research, he set off for Calabria in the south of Italy with a tape recorder to work on getting his accent absolutely right. Although the film was not very well received, De Niro's performance was picked out for special mention.

In 1970 De Niro appeared in his first commercial film, *Bloody Mama,* albeit a B-movie with a poor script. Director-producer Roger Corman liked mixing unknown talent with better-known actors, and Shelley Winters (playing Ma Barker, matriarch of a 1930s family of thugs) had helped De Niro get a role as one of her four sons. De Niro went into action, spending time in Arkansas, along with his tape recorder, to perfect the accent. The film itself was pure sleaze and was panned by the critics, but once again De Niro was picked out for his very realistic characterization.

Slowly his career was beginning to move. Shelley Winters advised him to join the Boston Theater Company to gain more experience, and this he did, achieving good reviews. His next part, in *Bang the Drum Slowly,* was for Paramount Pictures, and he had to undergo no less than seven auditions before getting the part. He played a baseball catcher who discovers that he has a progressive, malignant disease. Although it was not the lead role (the story was narrated by his character's best friend), he underwent rigorous training: first he perfected his accent, then spent several weeks learning all the tricks of baseball. Recognition came at last—his performance won him the New York Critics Award for Best Supporting Actor.

De Niro was now thirty. It had been a long haul, but he had never thought that anything would come easy, as his father's life, dedicated to painting and poverty, had amply demonstrated. Quietly and unassumingly, he continued his study of acting, never knowing if success was just round the corner.

De Niro as mobster henchman in Mean Streets

SUCCESS

A meeting at a party in the early 1970s was to change De Niro's fortunes. Martin Scorsese had grown up in Little Italy in New York's Lower East Side, very near where De Niro had lived; in fact they had met as children and when they met again they found they had much in common. Scorsese was an up-and-coming director. His latest project, *Mean Streets*, was set in the very streets where both had played as children. Their collaboration in this film would advance both their careers. Neither particularly liked the Hollywood system of having to have major stars to sell films. Scorsese was influenced by the French New Wave cinema, which focused on the whole film and the characterizations, and was not averse to using unknown actors. He invited De Niro to play Johnny Boy, a pathological maniac playing sidekick to a gangster (played by Harvey Keitel). De Niro knew the real-life "punk" whom Johnny Boy was based on. He talked to people who knew him, then used his own instinct to depict a streetwise character with a sort of rough appeal, but a loser. The film showed a new kind of realism—menacing violence in ordinary, seedy streets—but luridly lit to give them a threatening surrealism. Tony's Bar, where much of the action takes place, was in fact a film set thousands of miles away in Hollywood. The American public did not know quite how to take this new kind of realism, but De Niro's acting was hailed as "wild and strong" and "intensely appealing," and was praised for its "terrific pace and energy."

He was offered a part in Frank Coppola's sequel to *The Godfather*, as Vito Corleone—in other words, the part Marlon Brando had played so electrifyingly in the original film. It was a hard act to follow—or rather, precede—as this was to be the *young* Corleone seen in flashbacks. It needed research if De Niro was to play it with authenticity. Brando had given the *padrone* dignity, made him a family man. Coppola now wanted to redress the balance by highlighting his less attractive violent beginnings as a gangster, and it was De Niro's task to reconcile these differences. He watched Brando's performance in the original film over and over again to catch the nuances. He flew to Sicily, first visiting Palermo and then the small hill town of Corleone, the very heart of mafia country where it had all started. These experiences gave him the dimension of fear lacking in Brando's interpretation: he found the Sicilians covertly watching his every move. But it was reciprocal, for he was tape recording their conversations and memorizing their facial gestures and expressions. The resulting performance was dazzling, and he won an Oscar for Best Supporting Actor. Brando himself hailed him as "the most talented actor working today," but recognizing De Niro's self-effacing modesty, added: "I doubt if he knows how good he is."

De Niro was still living in a modest apartment in Greenwich Village and had a small circle of friends, mainly those he had met while acting. He fell in love with a young black actress, model, and singer—Diahnne Abbott, who, temporarily jobless, was surviving as a waitress. She had a six-year-old daughter, Drina, from a previous marriage. The romance developed gradually; she liked his quiet manner and his gentleness, and he was attracted by her commitment to her career. But it would blossom into a passionate relationship, although they were never possessive of each other and gave each other space.

After winning his Oscar for Vito Corleone in 1974, De Niro never looked back, apart from an unfinished project with Mike Nichols, *Bogart Slept Here,* about an out-of-work actor. Nichols found De Niro "undirectable," while De Niro found Nichols virtually impossible to work with. De Niro's next film, Bertolucci's *Novecento,* had a different set of problems. A straggling epic with a communist message, it recounted the parallel lives of two boys: one (De Niro) born to wealthy landowners, the other (Gérard Depardieu) a poor peasant. Friends at first, they find themselves in adulthood on opposing political sides and their friendship turns to hatred. The film suffered from "director's megalomania" (both Orson Welles and Maria Schneider walked out) and it became wildly overlong and overbudget, the director seemingly unable to stop his creative flow. Although De Niro admired Bertolucci's intensity, the two clashed, and Bertolucci found De Niro sensitive but neurotic (they did, however, became firm friends later). The heavily edited end product was unfortunately not a box office success.

De Niro's next project, Martin Scorsese's *Taxi Driver, was* a success, even though that too went over budget—by half a million dollars. Scorsese recalled being constantly hassled by the studios. A film about urban loneliness and a man who is driven crazy by it, it stars De Niro as ex-marine Travis Bickle, a shy loner who drives a cab by night, obsessively drawn to the city's night life. Increasingly appalled by the world he sees but too timid to indulge in it, he unleashes a torrent of sickening violence. De Niro's girlfriend, Diahnne, was given a small part, as a movie usherette. He, as usual, submerged himself in his role. When they were discussing how he should play his role, De Niro asked Scorsese, "What sort of animal would I be like?" Scorsese suggested, "Why not a tiger?" "No," De Niro said, "I think I'd be more like a wolf, always on the lookout, watching." So he went off to the zoo to study how a caged wolf behaved. Scorsese liked that—he has always liked actors who play by their instincts. De Niro also took to driving a cab at night for two weeks, only to find one fare recognizing him: "Wow! Last year you won an Oscar, and now you're driving cabs! Guess it's hard to find steady work."

The reviews were stunning. The film made over $25 million at the box office, and was nominated for four Oscars. De Niro played his part with utter conviction. His words "Are you talkin' to me?" as he addresses his lone reflection are now part of film history. One member of the public unfortunately became completely obsessed with De Niro's character, who at one time in the film stalks a presidential candidate. Watching the film over and over again, a man named John Hinckley came to think that he *was* Bickle, and he made an assassination attempt on the real president of the United States, Ronald Reagan.

De Niro in the title role of Taxi Driver

De Niro in The Deer Hunter

HOLLYWOOD

Despite De Niro's dislike for the razzmatazz of Hollywood, his next film would not only take him there, but would have Hollywood as its subject. Most of his supporting cast would be Hollywood stars too: Anjelica Huston, Jack Nicholson, Tony Curtis, Robert Mitchum, Donald Pleasance, and others. The film was *The Last Tycoon*, directed by Elia Kazan, who had been Brando's idol and who had done more than any other director of his generation to encourage method acting in the film world. De Niro did not want to miss the opportunity of working with him. De Niro and Diahnne moved to a rambling house in Bel-Air, having been banned from the hotel suite they were living in when it was discovered that Diahnne had smuggled four cats inside.

Kazan had a hunch that De Niro would be right as Monroe Stahr, the young workaholic movie mogul who burns himself out in his thirties. Sam Spiegel, the producer, who had invested $5.5 million in the film, thought otherwise: he saw De Niro as a common, "petty larceny punk" lacking social graces. Added friction was caused by the fact that Kazan found Harold Pinter's adaptation of Scott Fitzgerald's novel tedious and desperately in need of more action and love interest, and that almost everyone, except Sam Spiegel, found the leading lady's beauty outshone her acting ability.

For De Niro it was an entirely new, challenging sort of role and he worked himself into it by walking the deserted lots at Paramount Studios in a three-piece suit and thinking, "This is all mine." He dieted—losing over forty pounds—to make himself look ambitiously thin. But, in the end, his part had little impact—he was too low key, and the love interest was weak.

Not so in his private life, for in June 1976 De Niro and Diahnne married quietly, in the presence of just a few friends. Diahnne was pregnant, and their son Raphael (named after the Rome hotel where they had vacationed) was born during the shooting of De Niro's next film.

The Last Tycoon had not been a commercial success and a change of image was required. His friend Scorsese invited him to take the supporting role in a musical, *New York, New York*, set in the 1940s. His stage wife was the dynamic Lisa Minnelli, seduced into a rocky marriage where, though both husband and wife are madly in love, they just can't live together. They separate and there is a final nonreunion in which they both walk away. Diahnne also had a part as a beautiful singer. De Niro enjoyed his lessons to learn the tenor saxophone for his role, though his music coach didn't. De Niro had insisted on three months' intense study, asking so many questions that he drove his coach crazy.

In stark contrast to *New York, New York* was *The Deer Hunter*, Michael Cimino's attempt to show how the Vietnam War impinged on the lives of ordinary Americans, and in particular on a small community living near a steelworks. It depicts three men from that community drafted into the army and sent to Vietnam. They are captured by the Vietcong and subjected to horrendous torture, from which they suffer permanent emotional and mental damage. For six weeks De Niro went to live in the steel towns in Indiana, West Virginia, Pennsylvania, and Ohio, eating, drinking, and playing pool with the men, though none of the steel mills would allow him in to work. Shot in Thailand, the film almost occasioned an accident when De Niro and fellow actor John Savage had to hang onto a helicopter thirty feet above the river Kwai, before falling into the water. The helicopter flew too low and took out a bridge, with the actors still clinging to it. Meryl Streep agreed to take a small part in the film because her boyfriend John Cazale was playing one of the three men. Sadly, Cazale had bone cancer and died before the film was released. Streep's part was enlarged and she played romantic scenes with De Niro. Each was impressed by the other's professionalism.

De Niro is a pivotal figure in the film and he felt it was the best performance he had ever given. He was nominated for an Oscar and the film was voted Best Motion Picture of the Year. However, as a realistic picture of Vietnam it was sadly biased, and at the Berlin Film Festival, the Eastern bloc countries walked out: to them the film was an insult to the Vietnamese people.

In the spring of 1979, De Niro and Diahnne separated. Part of the problem was that De Niro was hardly ever at home—he spent much of the time away immersing himself in his various roles, and when he was at home the intensity of his role playing made him extremely difficult if not impossible to live with. Diahnne had also decided that she actually liked Hollywood, whereas De Niro could not even bear to turn up for the Oscar ceremony. She now felt caged in by his obsessive need for privacy. While she stayed in Hollywood, De Niro returned to New York, although they would continue to see each other and share holidays with the children. The marriage breakdown hurt him intensely. He told a friend that he could have been just as happy without the fame. "I miss Di and the kids terribly. They are always on my mind." But by this time De Niro had become involved with another woman, a black model named Toukie Smith.

De Niro as Jake La Motta in Raging Bull

LOVE INTEREST

Jake La Motta, known as the "Bronx Bull," became World Middleweight boxing champion in 1949, then lost to Sugar Ray Robinson and went into a decline, ending up as a nightclub bouncer and comic. De Niro happened to read his autobiography and suggested it as a film to Scorsese. "I was interested in fighters," he said. "The way they walk, the weight thing—they always blow up—and there was just something about La Motta . . . I wanted to play a fighter— just like a child wants to be somebody else."

This he would do in *Raging Bull*. It was truly challenging and required concentrated training. La Motta himself coached him—over four months they played a thousand rounds, so that by the time they came to shoot the film, La Motta declared that De Niro ranked in the top twenty middleweights in the world, and La Motta showed the freshly broken caps of his front teeth to prove it. La Motta's ex-wife found an uncanny resemblance between De Niro and what had been her youthful husband.

La Motta gone-to-seed in the second half of the film demanded a totally different portrayal. Filming was delayed while De Niro flew to Italy and fattened himself into dissolute middle age by stuffing himself with pasta—he put on sixty pounds and developed a bullneck. Such was the transformation that his daughter Drina was ashamed to be seen with him. Shot in black-and-white, the film marks the high point in De Niro's achievement as an actor. Some may dislike it for its roughness, but no one can deny its power and lack of compromise. By comparison, Stallone's Rocky looks almost soppy.

When filming was over, De Niro felt depressed and did not work for a year. He flew to Italy for a rest, but was held for questioning at the Rome airport when an official mistook him for a terrorist. After he returned to New York, he saw an attractive woman in another car at the traffic lights one evening and decided to follow her. She was Helena Springs, a black singer who had done backing vocals for Bob Dylan, Eric Clapton, David Bowie, and Elton John. Their chance encounter developed rapidly into a passionate affair and lasted off and on until 1992, when it ended on a distinctly sour note.

De Niro's next role was a far cry from his previous one: he played a worldly priest whose love of success outweighs his love of the church. His religious adviser on the film thought his portrayal "the most authentic priest ever seen on screen." Robert Duvall played his brother who has become a detective. But the public was apathetic about the film. *True Confessions* was shot in Los Angeles, where De Niro renewed his friendship with the star of *Animal House,* comedian John Belushi, who idolized him. De Niro was with Belushi at his bungalow shortly before he died, and De Niro was devastated by the death of his close friend.

It was ironic that the subject of De Niro's next film should be about a would-be comedian, *King of Comedy,* made under Scorsese's direction again. De Niro plays a fan who desperately wants to escape his mundane existence and become a star. He succeeds in kidnapping a TV show host for a vital quarter of an hour while he performs his comedy act. And although taken off to prison, he writes his autobiography and achieves fame. Jerry Lewis played the TV host and thought De Niro "the ultimate professional." De Niro refused to eat lunch with Lewis during filming because their characters were quarreling in the film. Many thought De Niro too good for this part. The film cost $20 million to make but was a turkey. In the meantime Helena had had a baby, whom De Niro would adopt—Nina Nadeja De Niro. But he was still married to Diahnne and as yet there was no question of a divorce; in fact she was working with him in *King of Comedy*, as his character's occasional girlfriend.

For his part in *Once Upon a Time in America*, directed by Sergio Leone, De Niro was reputedly paid $2 million. The film tells the long saga of gangsterdom in America from the 1920s to the 1960s, and to give it authenticity, it was agreed that the same actors should play themselves at twenty, forty, and sixty years old. But it was a lumbering, meandering film that ended up wildly overlength and overbudget. The editing job performed to make it into a commercial-length film marred it.

In *Falling in Love*, also released in 1984, De Niro had a chance to act once again with Meryl Streep. The story, set in a New York bookshop, concerns a suburban husband and a suburban wife who meet, fall in love, and have an affair. Like the film *Brief Encounter*, which it resembles, the ending is unresolved. This was one of the few occasions in which De Niro played a romantic lead, and although both he and Streep gave sensitive performances, his character lacked the edge of the more macho roles his fans had come to expect, and they were disappointed.

De Niro had now entered his forties, a testing time for any actor. The next decade promised to offer the actor good parts.

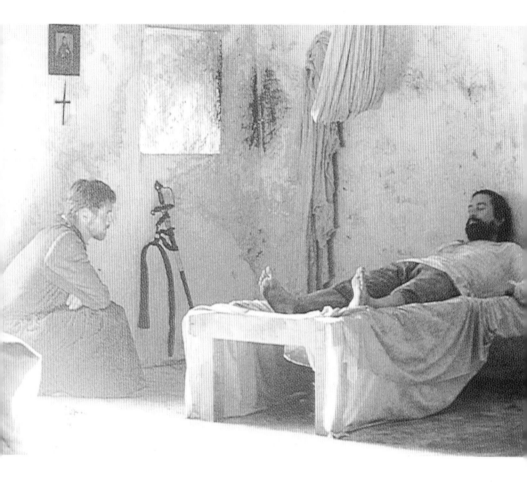

De Niro as Mendoza with Father Gabriel in The Mission

LIVING ON THE EDGE

Although only one film in which De Niro took part in in the late 1980s was a raging box office success, each of the characters he played showed his increasing diversity and range as an actor.

De Niro was a fan of the Monty Python comedy team, so when one of them, Terry Gilliam, was about to direct what he described as an "Orwellian pantomime," De Niro thought it might be fun. *Brazil* was a satirical view of the future, showing a world controlled by machines and bureaucracy. Bravely, De Niro was to play only a cameo role—as a repairman—while Jonathan Pryce played the lead as a victim of this futuristic nightmare. But the film was fraught with problems and friction between producer and director. The result was not a happy one, and De Niro's image, after yet another box-office failure, was at a low ebb.

After this came a nightmare of another sort: Colombia— the grueling setting for Roland Joffe's flawed masterpiece, *The Mission*, with a script by Robert Bolt. It was set in mid-eighteenth-century South America, at a Jesuit mission in the jungle. Joffe cast De Niro as Mendoza, a slave trader who converts to Christianity and becomes a Jesuit priest, only to convert back to his former violence in a bid to save the native Indians from the Spanish terror. Joffe said of De Niro's performance: "There wasn't anybody who had the inner complexity that Bob had [which] is there without him having to do anything—it's a part of his presence." De Niro grew his hair long and straggly for his part, and also sported a beard, which mightily impressed the native Indian extras.

They were on location for three months, and almost all the cast and crew came down with amoebic dysentery. The set was built above the breathtaking Iguaza Falls, but unfortunately it also turned out to be right in the path of a major cocaine-trafficking route out of the country, so they were constantly surrounded by police patrols with machine guns. On top of this they had to contend with stifling humidity, violent downpours, and flooding. The final scene, in which the mission is set ablaze, was more real than intended: the set caught alight prematurely, forcing some of the crew and cast to run for their lives, and the look of horror on their faces in the film was absolutely genuine. Problems also arose when the acting styles of De Niro and costar Jeremy Irons appeared to be incompatible. But after a while they came to appreciate each other's differing points of view. Irons described his fellow actor as "a lovely man."

The Mission won the Palme d'Or at Cannes Film Festival in 1986, but attracted very mixed reviews, ranging from "truly embarrassing" to "a magnificent achievement." Basically the film was far too long, and Warner Bros. lost a lot of money. The film did, however, bring De Niro more fame, and his next role seems at first a somewhat bizarre choice—a cameo part in *Angel Heart,* a supernatural thriller, complete with voodoo and murder, set in New York's Lower East side in the 1950s. De Niro plays the Devil himself, masquerading as Lou Cifre (Lucifer), and plays him convincingly down to the last long fingernail. Director Alan Parker was filled with admiration for De Niro's thorough approach and for his "phenomenal involvement" but thought working with him through a whole film might be an "exhausting" experience. The result was sinister and gory rather than entertaining and the public's reaction wasn't favorable.

After this De Niro took part in a stage play, *Cuba and His Teddy Bear*. He had not played in the theater for some ten years; he found it a restorative process and gave spellbinding performances. He was now ready to tackle the film world again, and this time his old colleague Brian De Palma came up with a winner. De Niro would play Al Capone in *The Untouchables*, with a screenplay by David Mamet and costars including Sean Connery and the then almost unknown Kevin Costner. Everyone was anxious to avoid the Hollywood cliché of showing gangsters as glamorous people, and the part of Al Capone demanded subtlety. De Niro read all he could find on the subject and watched the few old newsreels in which he appeared. In order to get his physical appearance right he went on another trip to Italy to fatten up again, and shaved the front of his hair to look as though he was balding. In real life Al Capone was a psychopath subject to violent temper tantrums, but he was also a charmer and an efficient businessman. As an example of his obsessive perfectionism, throughout the filming De Niro wore silk underwear, like Al Capone did; although it was invisible at all times, he said it helped him to feel like the man he was characterizing.

When the film was released, critics recognized De Niro's genius, describing him as "mesmerizingly intimidating" and "icily murderous." Sean Connery received equal praise. In a rare press interview, De Niro described how he enjoyed playing evil men—they seemed more plausible and real, and they lived life "at the edge."

De Niro transformed himself into Al Capone in The Untouchables

AWAKENINGS

The late 1980s marked a period of changing priorities for De Niro. In 1987 he was invited to the then–Soviet Union to head the jury at the Moscow Film Festival. As a remarkable symbol of rapprochement, the festival opened with a showing of *The Deer Hunter,* and De Niro was at pains to explain that it was an antiwar rather than an anticommunist film.

In the spring of 1987, Toukie Smith, who had remained a secret girlfriend of De Niro's for some eight years, was mourning the death of her brother, the fashion designer Willi Smith, who had died of AIDS. In a loyal move, De Niro agreed to participate in a TV information advertisement on AIDS.

Before his Moscow trip, De Niro was asked to play in a commercial comedy, *Midnight Run*, produced and directed by Martin Brest of *Beverly Hills Cop* fame. Handcuffed to costar Charles Grodin, De Niro plays a bounty hunter returning a Mafia bookkeeper to Los Angeles after he has embezzled his *compadres'* funds. Grodin had confessed to a phobia of airplanes, so the hilarious, cliff-hanging journey is undertaken by train, bus, and car, with a bunch of thugs in hot pursuit. The film was a hit and De Niro said he had great fun making it.

He then returned to New York to begin working seriously on a project he had had in mind for some time—to create

De Niro with Charles Grodin in Midnight Run

his own film center and restaurant in TriBeCa, the downtown neighborhood where he now lived. Once an inner-city zone of factories and warehouses, it was fast becoming a fashionably artistic quarter. Although he was said to have been netting as much as $5 million a picture, having his own film company would not only offer him artistic control, but would also give him a greater percentage of the profits. Others had tried this in the past—years before Marlon Brando had found it was not as easy as it looked, but more recently stars like Robert Redford, Bruce Willis, and Sylvester Stallone had made a great success of their ventures. It would take De Niro several years to get his idea off the ground. Although he was very comfortably off, it needed vast funding.

He and Diahnne had still not divorced and he was now contacted by Helena Springs again. Although he had adopted her daughter Nina, he had only seen the child once and had not offered any financial support. Helena had married and her husband, who loved the little girl, desperately wanted to adopt her. De Niro refused, and also refused to contribute any funds toward her education, or to behave like a father to her.

Just as there was confusion in his private life, so his film career became directionless. He was a star who, because he stuck to his artistic values, did not fit easily into the system— certainly not the Hollywood system at any rate. He took part in a number of inferior films, including *Jacknife*, an attempt to show the aftereffects of the Vietnam War on a veteran who cannot adapt to normal life. It was a plodding film and many were surprised that he had accepted a role in it, but assumed he had seen it as a kind of echo of *The Deer Hunter*. Perhaps De Niro was anxious to raise funds for his TriBeCa project, and his next film, a remake of the 1950s comedy *We're No Angels*, was probably taken on for the same reason.

After this he was able to become one of the buyers of a warehouse on Canal Street near his home, for $7 million.

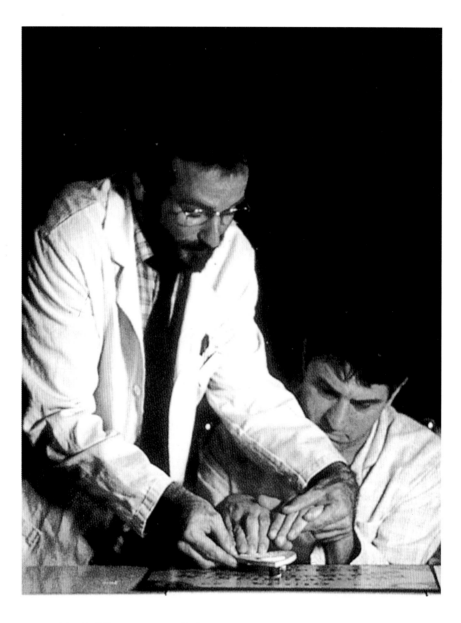

Robin Williams attends his patient De Niro in Awakenings

Another twenty-three investors came up with almost $3 million more, although he still needed much, much more to turn the warehouse into a going concern as part of his TriBeCa project. Although the money was welcome—and needed—De Niro did not court big parts in commercial blockbusters just for the sake of money; far more important to him was the interest of the role, particularly if it offered a completely new experience. Penny Marshall's film *Awakenings* presented just such an opportunity. It was based on Dr. Oliver Sacks's account of a real-life experiment on Parkinson's Disease patients in a mental hospital who had sunk into a rigid, catatonic state, but who, when given the medication L-Dopa, suddenly emerged from their paralysis and began to talk and move around. Then, as the effects of the drug wore off, they once again reverted to their frozen postures and frozen minds. De Niro took the part of a patient, Leonard Lowe, while Robin Williams played the psychiatrist. De Niro's character is played completely without expression or eye contact, until he is suddenly brought to life by the drug in an awesome moment. *Awakenings* was filmed in a Brooklyn mental hospital, and although it was a sentimentalized version of real events and was given an unreal, happy ending, it was nonetheless extremely powerful and moving, and did nothing but enhance De Niro's reputation.

Also in 1990, after ten years apart, De Niro and Martin Scorsese decided to collaborate on a new film, *GoodFellas* (the tale of a real criminal named Henry Hill, a New York *mafioso* who decides to turn state's evidence, and who, as a witness, is helped by the FBI to go into hiding). Nicholas Pileggi, who had written Hill's biography, collaborated on the screenplay. Many members of Scorsese's old team were brought together for this production. Hill was played by Ray Liotta, while De Niro played a supporting role as Jimmy Conway, a cold-blooded assassin, although, as usual, his role became pivotal. It was a violent film, and though not wildly received at the time, it has now come to be recognized as exceptionally good.

De Niro, now in his mid-forties, then starred with Jane Fonda in a film variously called *Stanley and Iris* and *Letters from Vietnam*. He plays a worker in a cake factory who is sacked because he cannot read or write; Jane Fonda acts as his teacher. Implausibly, Stanley then becomes a successful businessman and asks Iris to marry him. The film was not successful at the box office.

De Niro now faced new problems. Although the film center project was going ahead, he had to contend with picketing neighbors who were worried about the adverse effects his project might have on the locality. In addition to this, Helena Springs had divorced, and once again asked De Niro to take some part in their daughter's life and to start behaving like a father. Although he did make some provision, at this stage he still took little interest. In the meantime Diahnne was quietly pursuing their divorce, while a new girlfriend had made her appearance: supermodel Naomi Campbell.

De Niro in GoodFellas

De Niro and his screen son, Francis Capra, in A Bronx Tale

MAKE OR BREAK

At the beginning of the 1990s, De Niro earned nearly $20 million for six fairly indifferent films. *Guilty of Suspicion* was set in 1950s Hollywood, at the time of Senator Joseph McCarthy's witch-hunt of communist sympathizers. De Niro plays a blacklisted actor. In *Backdraft* in the same year, he has a supporting role as a fire investigator. While making *Backdraft* De Niro renewed his relationship with Helena Springs, who now wanted De Niro either to behave like a father to their child or to get out of her life. This ultimatum would have sad repercussions, but for the moment he refused to decide one way or the other.

Cape Fear, a remake of a 1962 film of the same name, was to be a joint production by Steven Spielberg and De Niro's own company, TriBeCa. Spielberg had to pull out, so Martin Scorsese took over the direction. De Niro, however, retained a fair amount of control, but by then the plot had already been forced into an unsuitably commercial mold. It is generally agreed that De Niro's performance was overdone. His next production, *Mistress*, was one of his least memorable and sank without trace.

Early in 1992 De Niro began to take a real interest in Helena's daughter, Nina. He invited her to Vancouver for a weekend and afterward phoned her frequently. Ten-year-old Nina was thrilled that at last she was getting to know her father. But Helena wanted the relationship to be put on a firmer footing.

In the meantime, De Niro made another film—*Night and the City,* another remake—using his own production company. The film was about wrestling and was not a wild success. His next venture—*Mad Dog and Glory,* about a police photographer—was also generally regarded as second-rate. The consensus was that he was taking on too many small-budget pictures, and making them too quickly. His next picture, however—*This Boy's Life*, for Warner Bros.—was better. It was directed by Michael Caton-Bell, who had directed *Scandal.* De Niro played an autocratic stepfather to a delinquent son, and Caton-Bell could not get over the intense perfectionism with which De Niro approached a role—for instance, trying on two hundred jackets to find one that felt just right.

But the tide was beginning to turn against De Niro: he was not expanding his range the way some of his fellow actors had, like Dustin Hoffman and Jack Nicholson. Instead, again and again, he drew inspiration from his New York background. He went on to direct and star in *A Bronx Tale,* the story of growing up in an Italian community in the Bronx, where old-fashioned values clash with the crime world. He gave his usual impeccable performance—as a bus driver this time—but directing was fraught with problems. Originally Universal Pictures was backing the film, but because of De Niro's meticulous approach it ran over budget. His own company was then obliged to take over the production and find new backers, but it continued to go wildly over even the new budget—creeping up from the original $16 million to $24 million and ultimately producing nearly four miles of film for editing. *A Bronx Tale* had its first showing at the Venice Film Festival that spring to a standing ovation. It lost money but was well received by the critics, and showed a new dimension to De Niro's skills.

In May 1993, when De Niro was fifty, his father died. De

The Creature in Mary Shelley's Frankenstein

Niro had genuinely cared for him, even hanging his paintings in his restaurant, and father and son had often been seen eating there together.

That same year De Niro also became the Creature in Kenneth Branagh's *Mary Shelley's Frankenstein*. Both Branagh and De Niro wanted to veer away from earlier film versions and follow Mary Shelley's concept—"horrific but capable of inspiring sympathy." De Niro also wanted the film to be intelligent and angry, and spent nine months preparing for the role. But the overhyping put off the critics and public alike; in the end it did little for De Niro's reputation.

De Niro was back on course with the release of *Heat*. Stylishly directed by Michael Mann, this "urban Western" follows an obsessive detective (Al Pacino) in his relentless hunt for McCauley (De Niro), a cold-blooded gangster. De Niro and Pacino make an effective duo in an albeit implausible scene when they sip coffee together (supposedly based on a true incident), followed by what must be the longest and loudest shootout ever. Having vowed that there will be nothing in his life that he can't walk away from in thirty seconds, McCauley proves it, with the subtlest and briefest of hesitations, by leaving his girlfriend to walk into the detective's final trap. The film ends on a highly sentimental note as the dying McCauley holds hands with Pacino's character in what must be the ultimate symbol of male bonding.

Scarcely a month after *Heat* came *Casino*, directed by his old friend Martin Scorsese, and using scriptwriters and some of the actors—like the brilliantly sinister Joe Pesci—straight from *GoodFellas*. *Casino* reflects the last blast of organized crime before Las Vegas turned its attention to becoming a family-friendly sort of place. De Niro plays Ace, the Mafia casino boss who falls for a high-class hustler (played by Sharon Stone), only to lose her to his murderous friend (Pesci). De Niro, Pesci, and Stone all give brilliant performances, even if the backdrop may seem to be set on familiar ground. Three new films starring De Niro appeared in 1996, *The Fan*, *Marvin's Room* and *Sleepers.*

As De Niro continues making films, will his performances continues to break the mold? Or will his future turn now more toward directing? On that, and on his private life, De Niro remains as silent as ever.

FILMOGRAPHY

The year refers to the first release date of the film.

1966	*Trois Chambres à Manhattan*	1986	*The Mission*
1968	*Greetings*	1987	*Angel Heart*
1969	*The Wedding Party*	1987	*The Untouchables*
1969	*Sam's Song*	1988	*Midnight Run*
1969	*Hi, Mom!*	1989	*Jacknife*
1970	*Bloody Mama*	1989	*We're No Angels*
1971	*Jennifer on My Mind*	1990	*Awakenings*
1971	*Born to Win*	1990	*Fear No Evil*
1971	*The Gang That Couldn't Shoot Straight*	1990	*Stanley and Iris (aka Letters from Vietnam)*
1973	*Bang the Drum Slowly*	1990	*GoodFellas*
1973	*Mean Streets*	1991	*Guilty by Suspicion*
1974	*The Godfather, Part II*	1991	*Backdraft*
1976	*Novecento (aka 1900)*	1991	*Cape Fear*
1976	*Taxi Driver*	1992	*Mistress*
1976	*The Last Tycoon*	1992	*Night and the City*
1977	*New York, New York*	1993	*Mad Dog and Glory*
1978	*The Deer Hunter*	1993	*This Boy's Life*
1980	*Raging Bull*	1993	*A Bronx Tale*
1981	*True Confessions*	1994	*Mary Shelley's Frankenstein*
1983	*King of Comedy*	1995	*Heat*
1984	*Once Upon a Time in America*	1995	*Casino*
1984	*Falling in Love*	1996	*Sleepers*
1985	*Brazil*	1996	*Marvin's Room*
		1996	*The Fan*

INDEX

INDEX